REPORT

OF THE

STATE BOARD OF EDUCATION

ON THE

PROPOSED SURVEY OF THE COMMONWEALTH.

Prepared by Order of the General Court.

BOSTON:
WRIGHT & POTTER, STATE PRINTERS,
CORNER OF MILK AND FEDERAL STREETS.
1874.

REPORT

OF THE

STATE BOARD OF EDUCATION

ON THE

PROPOSED SURVEY OF THE COMMONWEALTH.

Prepared by Order of the General Court.

BOSTON:
WRIGHT & POTTER, STATE PRINTERS,
CORNER OF MILK AND FEDERAL STREETS.
1874.

REPORT.

The Legislature of Massachusetts, at its last session, directed the Board of Education to inquire into the expediency of a new survey of the State. The undersigned, on behalf of a Committee of the Board, to whom the subject was referred, reports—

That on the fifth day of November, 1874, they invited a few scientific and other gentlemen, from different parts of the State, who possessed peculiar facilities for giving information upon the subject, to advise with them. The meeting was fully attended, and showed that a deep interest was felt in the subject. The remarks made by these gentlemen are submitted herewith. At the close of the hearing the Committee requested Profs. Peirce, T. Sterry Hunt, and Messrs. Shaler and Scudder to act as a committee, and, after a careful examination and conference with others, to present their views on the proper method of making the survey, its scale, the time required, and the probable expense.

The Committee desire to express their thanks for the very acceptable manner in which they have performed their work, and submit their report herewith.

The former survey of the State seems to have been inaugurated by a Resolution of the House of Representatives, in June, 1829, instructing a special committee of the House to consider the expediency of procuring a map of the Commonwealth. This committee reported in February, 1830, that such a map was necessary, and the next month a Resolve was passed by which Governor Lincoln was authorized to appoint a surveyor to make a general survey of the State upon trigonometrical principles, and project an accurate skeleton plan of the State, the external lines thereof, and the most prominent objects within these lines, and their locations. By a second Resolve the towns were required to make surveys of their territory at their own expense before January 1, 1831, and a fine of $100 was imposed on each town failing in the same, the fines to be added to the state tax assessed upon the delinquent towns. Succeeding Resolves authorized the employment of suitable persons to make a geological examination in connection with the general survey, and to procure a list of the mineralogical, botanical and zoölogical productions of the State. In 1837 the governor was authorized to make a further and thorough geological, mineralogical, botanical and zoölogical survey, with particular reference to the discovery of coal, marl and ores, and to obtain an analysis of the various soils of the State for the benefit of agriculture. A list of the documents of the General Court relating to the former survey is annexed to this Report.

These Resolves provided for a trigonometrical, topographical, geological and biological survey.

A trigonometrical survey determines, by astronomical and other calculations, the latitude and longitude of different points, which are marked by fixed natural or other monuments.

A topographical survey delineates the surface of the country, and on accompanying maps shows the location and elevation of the hills and valleys, the course of the streams, the water-basins, and all the ways, roads and buildings erected upon the surface.

A geological survey describes the rocks, minerals and soils of the State.

A botanical and zoölogical survey describes all that lives, animate or inanimate. The whole gives a complete account of the present condition of the world in which we live.

The portion of the survey performed by agents appointed by the governor was intrusted to men qualified for the work, and was well done. The astronomical calculations were made by Mr. R. T. Paine; the remainder of the trigonometrical survey was commenced by Mr. James Stevens, assisted by Mr. Simeon Borden, and after the resignation of Mr. Stevens, in 1834, was completed by Mr. Borden. The Coast Survey of the United States have since then made complete trigonometrical and topographical surveys of the entire seacoast of the State, including all of the counties of Suffolk, Nantucket and Dukes, the greater part of Barnstable, and portions of

Essex, Middlesex and Bristol. They resurveyed portions of the work of Mr. Borden, and found it correct and accurate. The trigonometrical survey of Mr. Borden, and the topographical survey of those portions made by the Coast Survey will not require to be repeated. Some of the secondary points determined by Mr. Borden, such as spires or other similar landmarks, may have been lost. Congress has provided that the Coast Survey shall determine the necessary triangulating points in every State which shall make appropriations for a topographical survey. It will, therefore, determine these points and also furnish whatever additional trigonometrical points are required for the basis of such a topographical survey as is now contemplated. The actual expenditure by the general government, in behalf of the State, will be so large a sum that the State may well take measures to obtain it. Besides this financial aid, there is a great advantage in having the skilled experience of the Coast Survey officers, who will execute this work, and the standard of accuracy thus secured to the State survey, and the opportunity afforded while this Act of Congress remains in force, should not be lost sight of in the interests of the State.

The topographical survey was made by the several towns. These generally employed local surveyors but little qualified for the work. Their surveys rarely gave more than the superficial area of the town, without reference to hills or valleys, while the scale adopted—one inch to two and one-third miles—was much too small to show the artificial, or even many of the natural features of the country. They would, therefore, have been of little value, even if correct; but they were often inaccurate, and being made by so many different parties, great discrepancies frequently existed between the surveys of contiguous towns. Consequently it was with difficulty that, from such material, any State map could be made. Unless such a survey is made under a single direction, by competent parties, and of a suitable scale, it cannot be of much value.

The map of the State was completed in 1840, and published in 1843. In 1860 and 1870, revisions were made, under Resolves, by Mr. H. F. Walling. No State aid was granted, but Mr. Walling was allowed to use the field maps and notes of his predecessors. The State map has been of little use in the construction of roads, railroads or water-works, or in geological research, or in the delineation of the water-sheds. As the natural features of a country do not change, if a topographical survey had been made at that time with the accuracy of the trigonometrical, only the addition of new artificial works from time to time would have been required.

The geological survey was conducted by Prof. Hitchcock, and at that time gave a better account of the geology of this State than had ever been given elsewhere in this country; but the science of geology has so greatly changed since then, that we are now informed that few States know less of their mineral wealth than Massachusetts.

The former biological surveys consisted of Reports made by Messrs. George B. Emerson, on the Trees and Shrubs; T. W. Harris, on the Insects injurious to vegetation; Chester Dewey, on the Herbaceous plants; E. Emmons, on the Quadrupeds; D. H. Storer, on the Fishes and Reptiles; A. A. Gould, on the Invertebrate Animals; and W. B. O. Peabody, on the Birds. Each of these gentlemen received $350 for his work.

The Reports of Messrs. Emerson, Gould and Harris are standard works, and probably of greater value than anything upon the subject written at that time. Harris's Reports have been twice republished; Gould's once. Emerson's are now out of print, but he has collected new material for another edition.

The agricultural survey was directed by the Rev. Henry W. Coleman, who made three excellent Reports between 1837 and 1840. They were confined to two or three counties in the eastern part of the State, but have been valuable manuals for farmers.

From this synopsis, it will appear how broad and comprehensive were the views entertained by the Commonwealth at that period, what was actually accomplished, where we are to take up the work, and what remains for us to do.

Topographical Survey.

The value of a topographical survey depends, in a great degree, upon its being of a suitable scale. The scale adopted in the ordnance survey of Great Britain, and the ordinary field scale of the Coast Survey, is six inches to the mile. This is considered the best, and several gentlemen who appeared before the Committee urged its adoption for the proposed survey. But the expense increases in an almost geometrical ratio with the scale, while the value of maps on a large scale is greater for cities and large towns, and those parts of the State where there are mineral formations, than for other sections.

The Committee of Experts, after mature consideration, recommend a scale of 1 : 25,000, or $2\frac{1}{3}$ inches to the mile. This would permit the delineation of contour lines twenty feet apart; but in order to reduce the expense, they recommend that exact measurements be taken only every one hundred feet, and that the auxiliary lines between them be filled in by the topographer on the spot; this will exhibit the hills and valleys, every river and stream, all ponds and reservoirs and other natural features, all forests and arable lands, common roads and railroads, and every building. Maps on a smaller scale can be easily prepared, and the expense of the preparation and publication would probably be repaid from sales to the public.

In some parts of the State, especially in the larger and more wealthy towns, the scale of six inches to one mile, or 1 : 10,000, should be adopted. This scale will furnish maps large enough to give the boundaries of every estate, in addition to the work on a smaller map. This survey can be performed by the State at less expense, better, and with greater uniformity than by the several towns. The Committee therefore recommend that in all towns of a given valuation, the survey on the larger scale be made by the State, and the extra cost be charged to the towns benefited, and collected with the annual tax.

The importance of a topographical survey on the scale recommended, for the laying out or changing the locations of roads and railroads, is too evident to need elaboration. The Committee were strongly impressed by the testimony of Mr. Adams, Chairman of the Board of Railroad Commissioners, on this point. Under the general railroad laws of the State, parties who wish to build a railroad are required to submit a survey of the route to the commissioners, for their approval. If it appears to be correct, and shows a feasible route, the commissioners are obliged to locate the road. Such a topographical survey and map as proposed would enable the commissioners to detect any inaccuracies in the survey submitted, and to select the most eligible route. Had such a map been made in 1833, it would not only have saved the individual survey of each railroad, but our roads would have been better located, with easier grades, and more economically operated. The town and county surveyors would also have used it in the location of every new road, and in the straightening of old roads, and thus many millions of dollars would have been saved to the Commonwealth. Nearly all the necessary main railroads are constructed, but many branch and lateral lines, and many new roads will still be needed, and for these the survey is important.

Hydrographical Survey.

Massachusetts can never be a great agricultural State; her prosperity must depend almost entirely upon her manufactures. For the success of these, abundant supplies of water are indispensable. Wherever water-power can be found in our State, it is the most economical agent for propelling machinery, and even where steam-power is used, a constant supply of pure water is equally necessary. The population of our State is rapidly increasing, but the growth is almost entirely confined to towns and cities. As they increase, the ordinary sources of water become insufficient and impure, and the water must be brought from abroad. It is therefore essential to know from what sources an adequate supply can be obtained. The average rainfall during the year, in different parts of the State, is well known. A part is lost by evaporation, or is absorbed by the earth; the remainder runs into our streams and rivers, and can be made available for our wants. The value of any supply of water depends mainly upon its being constant and uniform. This can only be secured by the construction of dams and reservoirs, and these, if properly located, can supply many factories, as all require the surplus water at the same time. By such means, the available water-power of Lowell has been increased, until it is three times as large as formerly.

The number of towns that are constructing or extending water-works is very large, and soon almost all our towns will rely on artificial supplies. The introduction of water necessitates the construction of drains and sewers to carry off the refuse water and deposits. This is discharged into natural water-channels and basins, and, without great care, will pollute the supply for other towns. The results of an improper system of drainage are already visible in many places, but especially in the vicinity of Boston.

The erection of certain kinds of factories on our streams also renders the water unfit for domestic use. The hydrographical survey will show all the water-courses, the water-sheds and drainage-basins; the total supply that can be relied upon in each district; also where dams and reservoirs can be safely constructed to store the largest supply of water. Such an undertaking will consider the interests of the whole people, and not of any one locality, and, at the same time, furnish a comprehensive survey, which will provide for the wants of every town, save the necessity of independent surveys, and give indispensable and reliable information upon all these questions.

The Geological Survey.

Within a few years the science of geology and the system of geological surveys have changed, and therefore the surveys of a generation ago are now insufficient. Plans are now prepared which exhibit the under-ground rocks, as well as those on the surface. Prof. Hitchcock, in his reports, several times referred to the very imperfect development of our mineral wealth, and to the probability that many mineral veins would be discovered; and, even within a few weeks, Prof. Richards, of the Institute of Technology, Boston, has discovered valuable deposits of galena near Newburyport, under geological conditions precisely similar to those of the rich deposits of lead in Colorado.

It has been long known that in the south centre of the State there are extensive coal measures; but as the coal is very hard and of an inferior quality for most purposes, and as the course of the veins and their faults are not known, they have not been worked. This coal is unusually free from sulphur, and is, therefore, of considerable value in the manufacture of iron. Deposits of various kinds of iron ore have been found in different parts of the State, and it is believed that this survey will develop our coal-fields and show the character of the various ores and the extent of the deposits. The manufacture of this iron will afford a market for the coal.

We believe, from evidence presented, that a geological survey will develop mineral wealth which will alone repay the entire cost of the survey. The field-work of a geological survey depends upon and follows the topographical; for, when the geological formation of one district has been determined, it is comparatively easy, by the aid of contour lines, to trace these formations into adjacent localities, as the layers of rock above and below will generally be found conformable.

Biological Survey.

The sciences of zoölogy and botany have each made great advances in the last forty years, and great returns may, therefore, be expected from researches in these departments. New insects injurious to fruits and vegetables have appeared in the State, and others are sure to follow. The phylloxera was carried from this country into France and Switzerland, where it has destroyed many vineyards, and it is thought it will be necessary to replant them with hardier vines from America. The Colorado beetle is drawing, year by year, nearer our own State. In Germany the government have directed inquiries to be made as to the best means of preventing its appearance, or of stopping its ravages. The canker-worms and squash-bugs periodically desolate our orchards and farms, and destroy annually enough to pay the cost of many surveys. In 1871, in Essex County alone, $10,000 worth of onions were destroyed by a minute insect,—a loss that a slight knowledge might have prevented.

A knowledge of the habits of insects is necessary to enable us to guard our fields and orchards against their attacks. Our biologists have already made many valuable investigations, but until these are published and generally known, they can be of little use.

The agriculturist draws information from the reports of the geological and biological surveys as to the soils in different parts of the State, where beds of lime, marl and peat may be found, and how they can be most economically worked, what are the best methods of tillage, and what plants thrive best in different soils. Such knowledge would give a new impulse to farming, restoring worn-out land, increasing the fruitfulness of the productive, and even planting with trees the sand barrens of Plymouth County, Cape Cod and Nantucket.

Cost of the Survey.

In several States surveys have been commenced and prosecuted for one or two years, then abandoned, and afterwards resumed with great additional expense. This has been either because the expense was greater than was estimated, or from a mistaken impression that the necessity of the survey did not warrant the outlay. It would be unwise in Massachusetts to undertake a new survey, unless prepared to carry it on to completion. The scale of the survey being determined, the expense can be estimated by reference to the Coast Survey and to recent surveys in other States. In preparing our estimate we have had the aid of Prof. Peirce, who for many years was at the head of the Coast Survey, and of Profs. Hunt and Shaler, who have each had much experience in state surveys, and their opinion is, therefore, entitled to great weight.

The cost will vary considerably in different parts of the State; but it is believed that the average will not exceed $25 a square mile, if the work is carried on without interruption and on a uniform plan. The time required will depend on the number of parties employed. It has been thought desirable, in order to obtain the best results, that not more than five topographical parties should be employed at once, consisting of a principal and deputy surveyor and chain-man. To determine accurate contour lines for every hundred feet, as proposed, will require the organization of a distinct levelling party, which will be sufficient to furnish all the required data to the five topographical parties. There are in the State about seven thousand eight hundred square miles, of which eight hundred and fifty have been surveyed by the Coast Survey, leaving nearly seven thousand miles to be surveyed, and, if five parties are employed, it will require fifteen years.

The total cost for the field-work of the Topographical survey will be	$175,000 00
The Geological survey will require $5,000 a year, ...	75,000 00
The Biological survey $3,500 a year, ...	52,500 00
The office expenses $4,000 a year, ...	60,000 00
Levelling party, $1,500 a year, ...	22,500 00
	$385,000 00

This will require an appropriation of $385,000, payable in fifteen instalments of $25,666 each. The office expenses will be for superintendence, a competent draughtsman, repair of instruments, preparation of maps, and incidentals. The office should, if possible, be in the State House, where it can be at all times accessible to members of the Legislature and the public generally. There will also be required for an outfit an additional appropriation of $5,000 for the purchase of instruments, and the necessary equipment for the different surveying parties and for the office.

The cost of the former trigonometrical survey, including the preparation and publication of the map, was upwards of $70,000. The cost of the entire survey was nearly $100,000. The assessed valuation of the State in 1831—the year subsequent to that in which the former survey was commenced—was $208,360,407.54, and in 1874 it was $1,794,216,110.69. A similar proportionate expenditure at the present time would amount to more than $861,000.

It has been suggested that a considerable portion of the topographical and other surveys might be conducted by the professors of our colleges and teachers in the higher schools, with the aid of their pupils, and that in this way the expenes might be reduced and the survey made a great educational institution. The Committee do not believe it advisable to adopt this suggestion. The survey of each department should be intrusted to a single skilled person, who should be made responsible for its faithful execution. He can call in from professors, teachers and students, from year to year, such aid as they can render, and thus successive corps of observers in every department of natural history may be trained, and these portions made more thorough and minute than would be possible with the sum proposed for each of these departments.

Although topographical, geological and biological surveys are, to a certain extent, independent of each other, yet the whole work is a unit, and the several surveys can be made under one management at less expense and much better, than if taken up at different times under different administrations. The Committee are of unanimous opinion that it is for the interest of the Commonwealth that such a survey as we have described should be made. The Committee have not considered any plan for carrying on the survey, believing that the Legislature can best decide that point. They would, however, call attention to the excellent suggestions of Mr. Scudder in regard to the organization of a bureau for the purpose.

There is probably no other State where there are so many scientists as in Massachusetts. The aid of most of these gentlemen will be freely, and, to a considerable extent, gratuitously given to the survey and in preparation of reports upon their several departments. Massachusetts owes her position in the forefront of the United States neither to her size nor to her population, but primarily to the character and education of her men and women, and secondarily to the great development of her industrial resources.

This survey will, we believe, reveal still further her hidden wealth, develop her external resources, and give new impulse to all her energies, thus enabling her in the future, as in the past, to lead the still increasing number of the United States.

GARDINER G. HUBBARD,
For the Committee.

BOSTON, December 1, 1874.

At a meeting of the State Board of Education, holden December 2, 1874, this Report was unanimously adopted by the Board.

REPORT OF SPECIAL COMMITTEE.

Gardiner G. Hubbard, Esq., Revs. A. A. Miner *and* Phillips Brooks, *Committee of the State Board of Education.*

Gentlemen:—The Committee requested by you to report what should be the scope of the proposed scientific survey of the State, and especially what scale should be adopted for a topographical map; what has already been done toward the construction of such a map by the United States Coast Survey; what remains to be done, and the probable cost of its completion,—respectfully report that they have consulted, as requested, with many scientific gentlemen upon these points, and beg leave to present the following statements:

First. The United States Coast Survey has already surveyed and plotted 850 square miles of Massachusetts, on a scale more than large enough for the purposes of the contemplated map. This includes the entire seacoast and the islands, and no further field-work will be required upon the same ground. The only expense needed would be to copy their results upon a uniform system and scale. Contour lines have been traced over this entire area.

The triangulation of the State was completed by the last (Borden) survey, and the points accurately determined. Some of the primary points, however, and most of the secondary, are probably lost; but, in virtue of general instructions already given by the government, all that is necessary toward triangulation will be done by the Coast Survey, as rapidly as the means for its prosecution are granted by Congress.

Second. Less than 7,000 square miles remain to be surveyed, including all the hilly parts of the State.

Third. The Committee recommend a scale of 1:25,000 (about $2\frac{1}{3}$ inches to the mile), for the manuscript map; of course, it can be reduced to any desired size for publication. This is sufficiently large to allow the introduction of every natural feature of importance and of every building, but it would be confused by an attempt to represent artificial boundaries; it will also permit the tracing of contour lines twenty feet apart, and these could be followed without difficulty. The Committee recommend, however, that careful measurements be taken only for contour lines about one hundred feet apart; auxiliary lines between these can be filled in with sufficient accuracy by a skilful topographer upon the spot; in this way, the cost of the survey would be materially decreased, while its value will scarcely be diminished.

The Committee suggest that it would be well if the survey were authorized by the State to construct maps on a scale of 1:10,000, or even greater, for such towns as desired it, the additional expense being met by these towns; the State would thus aid the towns just as the general government aids the State, and the townships would secure superior maps at a moderate cost.

Fourth. The expense, as well as the value of a topographical map will increase very rapidly with the scale upon which it is constructed. The Committee have taken this into careful consideration in expressing their judgment, and while they would gladly recommend a scale of 1:10,000, the ordinary field-scale of the Coast Survey work (did they not fear that the expense of its accomplishment would practically defeat an attempt to undertake it), they do not hesitate to say that a map upon a smaller scale than 1:25,000 would be inadequate to the requirements of science and public interests at the present day. They estimate that, by the strictest economy, the field-work, as here planned, could be done at a cost of $25 per square mile. This would require maintaining five topographical parties in the field for fifteen seasons. It is, however, exceedingly difficult to arrive at an exact estimate on this point, from the want of any precisely similar work elsewhere. In addition to this, an annual grant of $3,000 would be essential for office rent, draughtsmen, repair of instruments, and incidentals, while a special sum, of not less than $5,000, would be required for outfit.

Fifth. As regards the remainder of the proposed survey, the Committee believe that it can be conducted most economically if a similar length of time is given for its accomplishment; the larger part of the work could then be done by our best men, who would be willing to give a portion, but who could not give the whole of their time. There would be the additional advantage of enlisting the service of a much larger corps, so that each part of the survey could be intrusted to the one best fitted to undertake it. The greater part of the biological work would doubtless be done without any direct outlay by the State, if the authors of the reports were to receive a specified portion of the receipts from their sale. Conducted in this manner, not less than $5,000 per annum ought to be expended upon the department of geology, and $3,500 per annum on that of zoölogy and botany. This estimate includes the preparation of the reports and the work of the artist,—everything, in fact, but the bare expense of printing the results of the survey. The sales of the reports will, it is believed, cover the cost of their manufacture, after a comparatively small initial outlay.

In conclusion, your Committee urge that the industrial, educational and scientific interests of the State demand that the survey be undertaken, if at all, upon a comprehensive plan, and be prosecuted uninterruptedly to its consummation.

Respectfully submitted.

BENJAMIN PEIRCE, *Chairman*.
T. STERRY HUNT.
N. S. SHALER.
SAM. H. SCUDDER, *Secretary*.

BOSTON, November 18, 1874.

Commonwealth of Massachusetts.

HARBOR COMMISSIONERS' OFFICE, NO. 8 PEMBERTON SQUARE,
BOSTON, 17th December, 1874.

DEAR SIR:—I have carefully examined the report on the subject of the proposed State survey, which you have favored me with the opportunity of perusing.

The statements and estimates relating to the topographical department of the survey are well and carefully based, and seem to cover the ground as fully as estimates and plans can be applied to a new project.

The references made to the work and data of the Coast Survey are correct.

Very truly yours,

HENRY L. WHITING,
Chief of Topography U. S. Coast Survey.

GARDINER G. HUBBARD, Esq., *Cambridge, Mass.*

LIST OF THE DOCUMENTS OF THE GENERAL COURT

RELATING TO THE FORMER SURVEY.

1830. Governor's Address. House No. 37, Order of June 18, 1829; Report of Committee; Resolve for Topographical Survey; Resolve requiring towns to make surveys.

1831. Governor's Address.

1832. Governor's Address. Senate No. 6, Stevens's Report. Senate No. 12, Message of Governor; Stevens's Report.

1833. Governor's Address. House No. 36, Report of Committee on Geological Survey; Resolve for publication of Hitchcock's Report. House No. 58, Message of Governor; Reports of Stevens and Paine. House No. 60, Resolve for reimbursing towns (not passed?). House No. 62, Message of Governor and three Reports by Stevens.

1834. Senate No. 11, Reports of Stevens and Paine. House No. 23, Report of Committee; Resolve for new edition of Hitchcock's Report. House No. 44, Report of Committee; Resolve for further appropropriation. House No. 75, Report of Committee; Resolve concerning Trigonometrical Survey and further appropriation.

1835. Governor's Address. Senate No. 3, Borden's Report. Senate No. 26, Paine's Report. Senate No. 63, Resolve for distribution of Geological Report.

1836. Senate No. 11, Paine's Report. Senate No. 82, two Reports by Borden.

1837. Governor's Address. Senate No. 9, Letter from Hitchcock. Senate No. 80, amendment to Resolve for Agricultural Survey. House No. 23, Report of Committee; Resolve for Agricultural Survey. House No. 26, Report of Committee; Resolve for new Geological and Biological Survey; Letter of Dr. Gould. House No. 39, Secretary's Report on the expenses of the State surveys.

1838. House No. 52, Hitchcock's Report. House No. 72, Report of Zoölogical and Botanical Commissioners; Resolve for continuation of survey; Governor's Letter.

1839. Governor's Address. Senate No. 69, Report of Committee on Map. House No. 11, Report on cost of Survey.

1840. Senate No. 15, Coleman's Report. Senate No. 36, Coleman's Report. Senate No. 49, Report on cost of Map; Resolve for further appropriation. House No. 19, Borden's Report. House No. 54, Borden's Report.

1841. Senate No. 29, Report of Committee on Map; Resolve for further appropriation. House No. 9, Report on cost of surveys, with numerous accompanying documents.

1842. House No. 13, Report of Committee on Map; Resolve for its publication.

1843. Senate No. 46, Report of Committee on Map; Resolve for printing and distribution.

1844. House No. 47, Report of Committee on Map; Resolve for distribution.

www.ingramcontent.com/pod-product-compliance
Lightning Source LLC
LaVergne TN
LVHW011147110826
845150LV00008B/2565

* 9 7 8 1 4 1 8 1 9 1 6 6 5 *